GHOSTS
OF TRINIDAD
AND
LAS ANIMAS
COUNTY

F. Dean Sneed

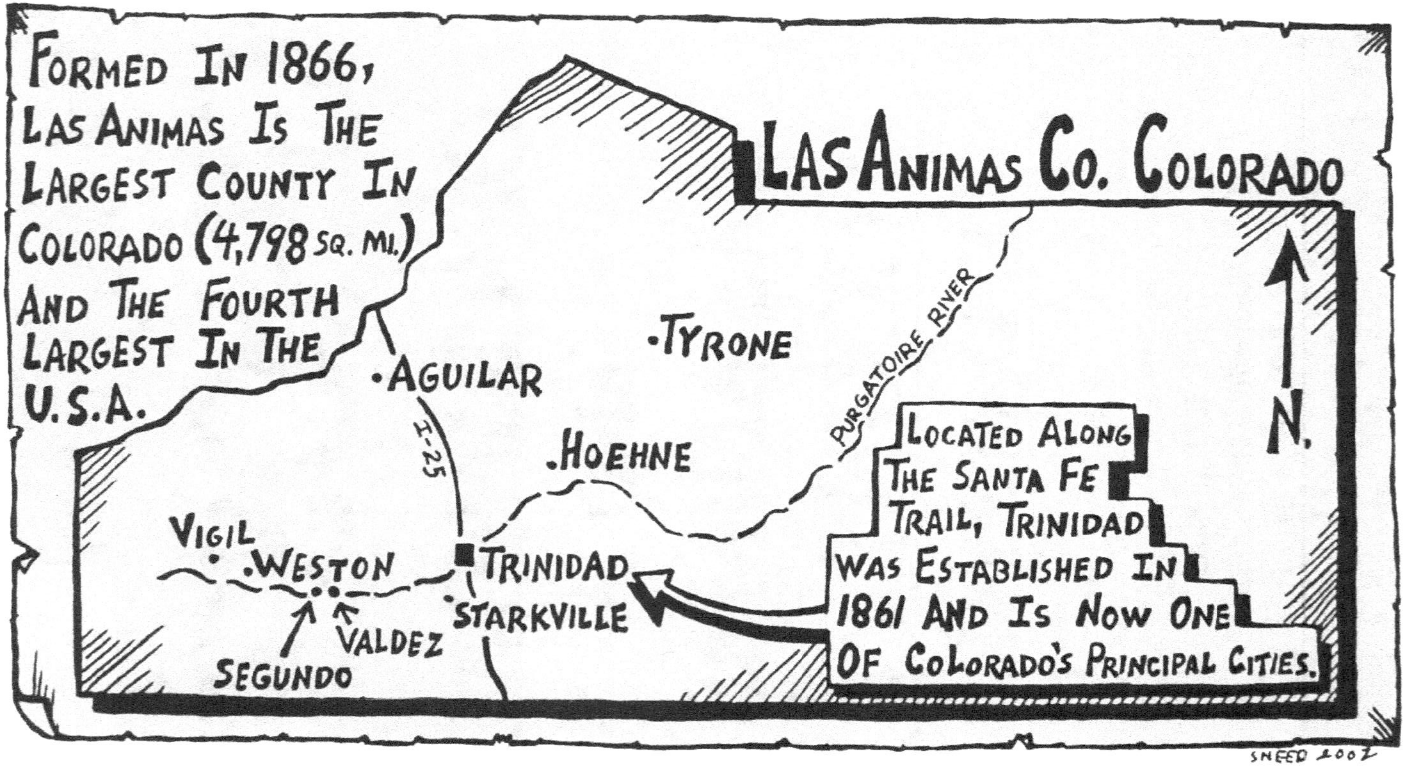

Formed In 1866, Las Animas Is The Largest County In Colorado (4,798 Sq. Mi.) And The Fourth Largest In The U.S.A.
Las Animas Co. Colorado
Purgatoire River
Tyrone
Aguilar
I-25
Hoehne
Vigil
Weston
Valdez
Segundo
Trinidad
Starkville
Located Along The Santa Fe Trail, Trinidad Was Established In 1861 And Is Now One Of Colorado's Principal Cities.
N.
Sneed 2007

CONTENTS

INTRODUCTION

This book is a collection of supernatural narratives, bizarre personal accounts, and eerie recollections as told by the people of Trinidad and, unless otherwise noted, Las Animas County.

You will find a wide range of strange phenomena within these pages. Everything from a restless statue (#13, "The Old Scout"), to a young woman's fearful meeting with a "lady" dressed in black (#39, "Death Came To See Her"), the poignant (#24, "The Crying of the Indians"), to the just plain weird (#27, "A Strange Piece ofCountry").

From historic homes to silent graveyards, wind-swept prairies to snow-capped peaks and misty valleys, almost every corner of Las Animas can claim a phantom or two. Some are mischievous, some sorrowful, and some still have the ability to frighten us out of our wits!

But no matter where the place, or what the apparition, these tales of unearthly happenings have one thing in common. All are entertaining and help to enrich the already colorful region in which we live.

F. Dean Sneed.

ACKNOWLEDGMENTS

I would like to thank the following for their kind help and patience: Diane Mason, Ray & Priscilla Opper, the Trinidad History Museum, the Carnegie Public Library (Trinidad), the Denver Public Library (Western History Department), the Trinidad Plus/Times Independent, the Trinidad Chronicle-News, the Denver Rocky Mountain News, various family members, and finally, a big thanks to all those who have contributed their precious time and priceless stories. Without you this book would not have been possible.

PART ONE:
SPIRITS
OF
TRINIDAD.

1. GRAVEYARD SHIFT

The courthouse itself, I honestly think, is haunted because there are so many different things... so many different sounds... that you will hear.

You could hear people laughing... I mean people actually laughing. And there was no one in the hallways. We used to have a big gate that would go across, you know, that would separate us from the regular hallway, and you could actually hear people walking, like coming down the stairs, talking and laughing. I used to think, "Well, I wonder how they got up there?" And there was no one there. The restroom, you know, a lot of times it was out of order at the police department, and we used to have to go all the way around the courthouse, on the inside [to the other restroom]. I would be walking, and I wore soft-soled shoes, I would hear hard soled shoes right behind me. Needless to say, I just kind of hurried along!

●●●●●●●

And talk about spirits, one time...and this is the truth and I'm not crazy...I had gone to work about two in the morning. They had had a DUI arrest and this young fellow...they had taken him upstairs [to the cells], because he couldn't bond out...and he hung himself. All the commotion had gone on before I got there. The off-going dispatcher briefed me on it and, from what I understood, the coroner had been there and everything had been taken care of. There was no one in there with me, because all the other officers were on the street. I heard a noise in the back room. I didn't think anything of it; I thought there was still an officer back there, maybe doing a late report. Then I heard someone kick a trashcan, or something. I thought, "What's going on back there?" So, I walked over and looked in and got this ugly feeling, because there was nobody back there. I walked back [to the front office] and I sat and I heard the trash can being kicked again. I thought, "There's something going on, there has to be somebody back there!" I went back and the trashcan was kicked over and pieces of paper were thrown out. I picked them up, put the trash can back, and I called an officer and told him about it. He sort of laughed and told me it was this one fellow's spirit come back to visit!

I was very uncomfortable that night. It wasn't the first thing that had happened here, it was just that I didn't know for sure if he [the young man] really did come back, or if whatever it was in the hallway, making all the racket, had just come in to play games. I don't know.

●●●●●●●

I didn't mind working graveyard shift, you know, because it was a fast shift. All the things that you had to get done, you got done and that was it. But certain times of the year, "they" liked to do rotten little things. I left my coffee on top of the windowsill, and had forgotten about it. My Sergeant came and told me, "Aren't you going to clean that up?"

And I said, "Clean what up?"

Someone had turned over my cup of coffee! I know I didn't do it; I always left my coffee there. If I had knocked it over I would have cleaned it up right away. I'm not a sloppy person.

Tablets *(notebooks)*, that we used to keep on top of the counter, were there, and then in the middle of my shift they were in the back room. I was the only one in there and I didn't take them back there. Strange things, like that, just didn't make any sense.

••••••••

Like I said, the thing at the courthouse that used to bother me the most was the laughter and the footsteps all over the place. It was uncomfortable when you heard it. You could hear them walk over to the gate and stop. Usually if someone was working late they would say, "Open the gate." I would get up, get the keys and open the gate. But during these times there would be no one there.

K. T. July 21, 2001

The Las Animas County Courthouse was designed by Architect I. H. Rapp in 1912. It was constructed by native craftsmen and built almost entirely of locally quarried sandstone.

2. OUR LITTLE GUY

We've had this house [on Colorado Avenue] for ten years and have been living here for eight.

The house had been empty for five or six years. Our friend's dad married the lady that owned it, so they were here up until that time. They really didn't do a whole lot with the house. We threw away tons of canned eggs, pickled eggs, pickled pig's feet, tomatoes, and stuff like that that didn't have the rings on them, just the tops. And it was like, "Oh, this is nasty!"

There was paper everywhere, old newspapers that we threw out by the tons. It was pretty bad. As a matter of fact, I thought it looked like the "Addams Family" house when I first saw it and I cried. I thought, "Oh my goodness, I don't know if I want to take on this responsibility!"

This was a five-bedroom house, whoever built it had a lot of money. The closets are good sized; you can actually put a chair in them. Back then if you could put a chair into a closet you were taxed for it. We could never find out who built the house, because they had a fire [at city hall] about twenty years ago and it burned the microfiche records. We can go back as far as the 1920's when this was a Pastor's house and he had his church down here on the bottom floor. So it was used as that for six or seven years.

●●●●●●●

The rest of the house was fairly warm...it had been sealed up; they had plastic on the windows...until you got to the dining room and it was cold. It was stone cold. Even the dog wouldn't come through it!

When we started redecorating is when our "little guy" showed up. We don't know who he is but his hair is just as white as my curtains. Whenever we're painting he shows up. When we put this wallpaper up a couple of months ago he was here. He doesn't harm anybody and when he thinks, or knows, that we're gonna start doing something...we're trying to clean out the basement right now...he walks up and down the hallway. It's weird because we're working downstairs and you'll hear noises upstairs. You can hear him walking. It's just like someone was pacing.

When we were insulating the basement, the little man showed up. He made sure that everything was done right. He'll brush by you, you know, just to make sure everything's okay. You'll feel like a breeze, he doesn't touch you; it's just a breeze.

He's about five feet tall or smaller, he wears work boots, the old kind that your grandfather used to wear, and fairly worn, baggy overall pants. He always has his hands in his pockets and he would be going (*nodding his head "yes"*), or he'll go like this (*shaking his head "no"*) and that's all you would see, just the back of him. His hands were always in his pockets, unless you miss something and his arm goes like this (*pointing*). He indicates where you missed a spot!

It's quite comical.

He's solid, you can't see through him and you never see his face. When you go to look again he's gone. You know, you're trying to do what you're doing without getting it all over yourself, and you look again and he's gone.

We see this little dog more than anything, or we'll hear the bell on his collar. I don't know what kind of dog it is, it's just white with short legs and a long tail. Our dog (*Button*) is white and buff colors, and about the same size. The dog kind of sticks around a bit and you can tell it's a dog. And it's not transparent either.

I'll be in the kitchen and [Button] will be in here (*the*

living room) and pretty soon I'll hear this pitter-patter. Without even thinking, I'll just toss something to her and she usually catches it. The meat will be sitting on the floor and I'll go, "Call the dog in here, she forgot her treat."

[My husband] will say, "She's still asleep!"

Button's fifteen, she can't hear, but there's nothing wrong with her snout. Once in awhile she'll wake up out of a dead sleep and start staring, but she won't bark. The funny thing of it is that she went deaf within six weeks after moving here. The vet says she's in excellent health. There's no heart problems, no lung problems, only a little arthritis. Still, if she gets a whiff of something that isn't right, she'll go through this house until she finds it. Then she comes back and looks at me like, "What did you do with it?" Then I know someone, or something, has been here. She's real perceptive.

●●●●●●●

We have things go missing and then about a week later they're back in a different spot, where I would never put them.

It does bother our daughter a lot. She was with us for two weeks and said, "I'm not sleeping down here by myself." My brother's the same way. He won't sleep down here by himself because, he says, something in this house bothers him.

As we get more familiar with everything around in the house, it doesn't bother us as much.

●●●●●●●

And now we have another "friend." [My husband's] dad passed away not too long ago. His dad's here, not all the time, but you can hear the front door open and he'll go, "It's me!" There's no question about it, because his dad has done that for, well, ever since we've been married. "Hey, it's me!" And you'll hear this little, like rap, on the door. If you don't lock it, the front door will open by itself. I'll tell [my husband], "Hey, your dad's here!" It's no big deal.

I don't know what's going on with the house, but I'd sure like to know who this "little gentleman" is!

J. M. /P. M. March 24, 2001

3. A BLAZING WHITE CROSS

One wintry evening in Trinidad, just after midnight, a gravedigger was working late at the old cemetery north of town. Pausing a moment to rest, he noticed two mysterious figures wandering aimlessly about the grounds. They both wore what appeared to be long, flowing robes and hoods. One was in brown, possibly black, the other in red with a blazing, white cross on his chest.

As the old man watched, he suddenly realized that his curious visitors were little more than skeletons wrapped in tattered cloth, floating above the headstones!

Thoroughly terrified, the gravedigger abandoned his work and hurried home as fast as humanly possible!

Anonymous source, 2002

4. GIGGLES

My house on First Street, it was quite something!

We lived in that house since I was in the third grade. You always heard noises and felt a cold chill up your back when you went to the basement. As I got older I raised my kids there. My oldest daughter used to talk to somebody up in her room. She's a special needs child, mildly retarded, so I just thought it was her imagination.

A couple of times [while doing] laundry in our basement, that's where [we kept] our washer and dryer, you would hear giggles down there and feel a cold breeze. And kids' clothes were always missing! You would buy something new for them and soon as you put it somewhere, it was gone. A month later you would find it in the oddest places, mostly downstairs. You would find it in a corner, or hanging over a chair that was down there.

●●●●●●●

And then it got to the point where we started seeing things. One night I was saying my prayers in bed before going to sleep. I had this picture in the hallway and you could see reflections into the restroom through this picture. I was lying there saying my prayers and I happened to look up and saw this little girl's shadow in the picture. She waved to me and faded into the wall!

A lot of people never believed me, until my boyfriend, who is now my husband, had come over when we first started dating. We were lying on the couch watching a movie and turned to each other and started talking. We turned back to the [movie] and the TV had changed to the "Spanish Channel." I said, "Did you change it?"

He said, "No, did you?"

I told him no, and then we heard a little giggle and little feet running across the dining room floor.

My oldest daughter always watched the Spanish Channel. She told me that her "friend" would watch it with her. I'm thinking that it's this little girl.

And then there was a time when he *(the boyfriend)* spent the night. We had thought my oldest daughter had gotten up and we told her to go back to bed. Within seconds [she] was on my side of the bed. I turned around and told him, "Oh God it's not [my daughter], it's that little girl!"

Needless to say, he got up and went home because he was terrified of it!

Another time, I was curling my hair and getting ready for a class. I heard a giggle in the bathroom and it got real cold. I got this real eerie feeling and I looked over by the tub. This little girl was standing there and I could see the outline of her body, but couldn't see her face. She giggled and faded away.

●●●●●●●

I was on the phone one night with my sister and the bed skirt to my bed...I was on the floor reading...just started moving back and forth. I thought our cat was under the bed, so I went and straightened out the bed skirt. I thought, "Well, maybe he was under there." I didn't see him, and it just started moving back and forth again.

Little things like that always happened. A kitchen chair

moved every now and then. The back door would [open and] close when you knew you locked it, lights would go on and off when you know you weren't doing it. I honestly think it was a little girl, because I had seen shadows of her.

My sister would never go over and visit me, she was always too afraid. Every time she did come over, that's when silly things happened even more. The door would all of a sudden slam. She would look at me and say, "Did you do that?"

"No. I'm sitting right next to you. How could I have done that?"

She'd get scared and say, "That's it, we're going home!"

You always heard the little giggle and feet running across the floor.

●●●●●●●

My ex-husband, when he lived there, got up one night as white as a sheet. I was sleeping with my kids, because he and I just did not get along, and he told me that I needed to call an ambulance. [I asked], "Why, what's wrong with you? You look like you're gonna throw up!" He said he felt like somebody was sitting on his chest when he was in bed, he just couldn't breath.

I went in [to the bedroom] and I didn't see anything or hear anything. I told him, "Go back to bed, you're gonna be okay." He had been drunk that night.

So, I sat up [the rest of the night] and I could hear the bathroom door open and close. I thought maybe he was sick, so I got up to check on him. He was still in bed and the bathroom door was closed. I went in there and I heard the giggle and I felt a cold breeze. I thought, "Oh great! She's probably torturing him because he was such a mean person!"

••••••

She never did anything harmful to me or the kids, just little weird things like hiding the clothes. You would hear her running through the house sometimes, because it was all hardwood floors. Our stairs were also hardwood at the time and you would hear her walking up and down the stairs.

When we were leaving, when we moved out of that house to come to Pueblo, it was full of sadness. It was just awful! The kids cried and didn't want to go. My son started crying because he couldn't find his toy, and my youngest daughter couldn't find her favorite doll.

My oldest daughter, she didn't want to go, period. She was madder than heck that she had to leave. Right before we left, we found the toys out in the middle of the dining room, where we mostly heard [the little girl].

Now my sister lives there, and she has never experienced anything!

A. B. August, 2001

5. WALTER

When I was buying the house [on East Second Street], at the time I really wanted it to have a ghost. I thought it would be fun, of course "Casper" is fun in the movies, but...Anyway, when I asked the lady who owned the house, who was also a real estate agent, if there was a ghost, she immediately looked at her daughter like, "Don't say a word, keep quiet!" She turned to me and said, "Oh no, this is a lovely home to live in..."

Immediately I knew there was a ghost in the house, just from their reaction.

●●●●●●●

The first night when I moved in, I wanted to get there earlier in the day, but I got there more like at dusk.

I thought my dog was going to love it. We opened the door, got her in, and she started crying. She walked around and she cried and cried. I said, "Oh Mattie, I thought you were really going to like the house!" I know that dogs sense spirits.

When we climbed up the stairs she started crying again. I thought she was going to be really happy there and she did [eventually] grow accustomed to the house.

One of the first encounters I had was on the very first night. I was very unsettled and I said, "Okay, if there really are people living here with me, I promise to make this house beautiful and I want you all to leave me alone. Don't scare me and we'll get along just fine."

I went to bed going, "Oh, I wonder if I'll get any sleep?" I slept fine until all of a sudden, at five o'clock in the morning, two lights in my bedroom went on. And they're the kind that you have to go and individually turn the switches. They both went on, bingo! At five in the morning. I said, "Okay, I guess we're all here, and if that's as scary as you get, it's okay with me!"

•••••••

I remember sitting, watching TV and I heard a crash. Bang! Glass shattering everywhere. I had put this lantern on the back of my toilet, for decoration, and when you flushed it kind of jiggled a bit. And I thought, "I should have known better than to put that on the back of my toilet!"

I heard all this glass going everywhere and I thought, "Ugh! I gotta go clean this up!" I go in there and it had fallen down, but it was in perfect shape, it was all in one piece.

Then one night I came home, and I have all those lanterns sitting on my mantle. I came home and it was dark. I didn't turn the light on, but I could see a little glimmer of light, something was on the floor. Again a lantern had been put on the floor. I still don't know what the significance of taking these lanterns and sitting them on the floor is all about.

•••••••

A gentleman that I was dating for awhile was house sitting [for me] when I was on a trip, and he heard a knock on the wall as you go up the stairs to the second floor. He thought, "Well, I'm going to knock back!" So, he went and knocked back. All of a sudden, the sound came again and knocked back at him. He just went flying out of the house and would not return to house sit until the next morning. My poor dog was there all alone!

Another time I was getting ready for another trip. It was summer time and I had shorts on, and somebody kept tugging at my shorts as I was walking up the stairs. I thought, "Oh, it must be my dog." My dog follows me everywhere. I turned around to tell her to stop it, and she wasn't there. She was already at the top of the stairs.

●●●●●●●

You know, I always thought that [the ghost] was Walter Bancroft, who owned the house. Walter was a distinguished businessman in Trinidad. He died on Christmas Eve *(1930)*. I just called the ghost "Walter," whether there was more than one.

When I first moved in, I had a bunch of psychics, a group of ladies, "cleanse" the house. Somebody thought they saw Walter. He was in the back, standing on the porch, smoking a cigar. In that same group, another woman saw a lady standing at these little windows in the bedroom. She just stands there all day and cries because she lost her baby. She waits for her husband to come home every night and she cries at the window.

I did not know that a little girl had also died there. I've had somebody pulling the hair on the back of my head and that makes me think that could be a little girl, you know, coming up and twirling my hair.

The first Christmas Eve I was there, knowing that Walter had died [on this evening years ago], I felt we ought to remember him, so I put out a plate of cookies. I didn't have any real cigars, so I laid out a bubble-gum cigar instead! I put something out to drink; I don't remember what, and some scented candles. I started to light the candle, then stopped. I thought, "That's real smart, light the candle and burn your house down while your sleeping!"

I woke up [the next morning] and there was this incredible aroma in my bedroom. It was just glorious! And I thought, "What is that smell?"

It was real dark and we were feeling our way downstairs to the kitchen...and the candle was lit! It was my conformation that Walter was definitely part of the house.

You know, since then I've thought about it, I light candles all the time, but I never get an aroma upstairs. That aroma was so intense!

●●●●●●●

A friend of mine and her husband came to visit. Of course they were intrigued by Walter, and all the Walter stories. They went to bed that night and they hadn't gone to sleep yet. All of a sudden their door just slammed shut on them. So, they got to meet Walter, and they haven't been back!

The only time I've been afraid [in the house] was when I was taking a bath and I heard heavy walking up the back steps. Boy, did I get out of the tub fast! I looked around the corner, and there was nothing.

I have never seen anybody in the house and would probably rather not! I don't mind the other things happening, but I think that would probably do me in.

I guess there was a fire once, and Walter appeared to two little girls that were sleeping there. They either lived there, or this was grandma and grandpa's house. The lady who stopped to tell my boyfriend [this story], said the little girls saw an old man who told them to get up and get out of there.

There was a fire in the house, I do know that. So there

could be some truth to that one!

●●●●●●●

I had a priest go to my house. We went to every room and he would sprinkle Holy water. He'd say, "How do you use this room?"

I'd say, "This is my office, this is my bedroom..."

He would bless every room individually. It was interesting, because I was dating a gentleman at the time and I hadn't told him that I was going to do that. He walked in the door and said, "Wow! This house feels so good! What did you do?"

That blew my socks off! I said, "I had the house cleansed today by a priest."

He said, "Boy, you can feel it!"

●●●●●●●

It was quiet for a good couple of years. In fact people have asked me, "How's Walter?"

And I'd say, "Oh, it's been real quiet. No stories to report."

But now I can report stories again.

I now have three dogs, and they're pretty much always around me. We heard an amazing crash upstairs one day. I thought, "I wonder what's fallen over, what caused that?" We all went upstairs, and didn't find a thing [broken].

Just yesterday, or the day before, again a big crash. You know, everybody gets startled and goes, "What is that?" It was in the front room this time. Again, not a thing [broken].

Then just the other day upstairs, the door slams again.

L. S. May 5, 2001

Said to be well over a century old the house, a two story "Queen Anne," was built...and is apparently still haunted...by its original owner, Walter Bancroft.

6. AN ELDERLY MAN

I worked at the mine at the time. Me and my wife were living at my mother-in-law's [on Colorado Avenue] because we were getting ready to move into our own house. I was sitting there waiting for a ride and fell asleep on the couch, when I woke up I saw a guy standing by the fireplace...an elderly man. It didn't really bother me, so I didn't think much about it.

Well, a neighbor...I was talking to him one day and I described this guy. And he said, "That man lived in that house years ago."

He had a little hat on, a green suit with a vest, a tie, brown pants, you know, like they wore in the 50's. I never knew him and I'd never seen him before. No one else had ever seen him but me.

A. R. April 2001

7. EVERY DAY THERE WAS SOMETHING

We didn't know anything about this house because we had traveled all the way from New Hampshire. We didn't even know [our landlady] when we got there. For two nights we were there by ourselves until we met her on the third day.

The very first night we stayed there, we experienced a little girl that called, "Mommy, Mommy." I asked my husband, "Did you hear that?"

He said, "No. If you heard something it must be the girls."

I yelled upstairs at the girls, this is like 10:30 at night, and they had gone to bed at eight. Nothing. So the next night, you know, our regular routine...10:30 go in to the bathroom, floss your teeth, get ready to go to bed. We heard the voice, "Mommy, Mommy." We both looked at each other and I said, "Did you hear it that time?"

"Yeah."

"Is that the girls?"

"No."

"Well, I didn't think so!"

It sounded like it was coming from the kitchen area. Either the kitchen or the "bulkhead" area. You go down in the basement, that's where we heard the voice.

●●●●●●●

My guinea pigs, when we first moved them in there I had them upstairs. You know how these old houses have the big coal vents? The guinea pigs, I put one near one of those vents and I put the other one on the other side of the wall. And my guinea pig, which would eat everything anytime you feed her, would not eat for two days. I couldn't imagine why she wasn't eating, this pig always ate! So I thought, "God, I wonder if something is in the vent?" So I moved her away and she started eating again. So that was kind of weird.

I had a cat that would not come downstairs. I had like eight or nine cats then, and one would not go downstairs.

My little dog would bark, running up and down the hallway. She would go from the kitchen door to the hallway and keep looking up and barking, you know, pacing back and forth. I have no idea what that was all about!

●●●●●●●

The basic part of this started happening within the first six months. It would happen all the time, not just once in awhile. Almost every day there was something.

We had things move around. The pictures [hanging on the wall] would move. There were three pictures, one in the middle and two on either side. In the morning they would all be mixed up. The chandelier would swing, and this would be at Halloween time. We had the house all dressed up and everything. We were putting up decorations, and I think it was the next day, that the chandelier was swinging in the living room.

Cupboards would bang at night. If I would yell at the girls, you know, if they'd get too loud, "You girls stop it!" or,

"Go to your room!" Then I'd hear this voice "mimic" me during the nighttime. It used to wake me up and I'd say [to my husband], "Did you hear that?" Sometimes he did, sometimes he didn't.

My husband was in the bathroom downstairs and we were all watching TV. He came out and goes, "All right, who was the smart-butt?"

"What are you talking about?"

"Who was knocking on the bottom of the door?"

"Nobody."

"One of you must have been playing around, knocking on the bottom of the bathroom door when I was in there!"

"No we hadn't. God strike me dead, nobody went over there and was knocking on the door!"

I don't know, just weird things.

●●●●●●●

It started the very first night we stayed there. We hadn't met [our landlady] yet. We met her on the third night and I told her what happened. We were all standing in the dining room and we all got chills, just because of what was said. I don't know if "something" was there or not. She had some "séance people" come over and they "cleansed" the house. They told my husband not to go downstairs after they cleansed because this "spirit" was so-called "living off his energies."

They said that there was a little girl locked down in the bulkhead area, because there was a whipping post downstairs. They thought that this little girl had died either on that whipping post, or on the back steps going outside from the cellar.

Originally they said there was a person by the name of "Henry." They didn't know if it was a first or last name, but he was of German descent. One of the séance ladies called back and she said, "Don't be alarmed, it's not a bad spirit. There are many spirits in there, but Henry stood out."

●●●●●●●

[My husband's] mother had passed away in January. Not long after that, this white figure came to the foot of our bed. [My husband] saw it but I didn't. He opened his eyes and was like, "Oh my gosh, what is that?" We don't know if it was his mom or what. It was there and all of a sudden, you know, it just disappeared.

That's the only visual-type thing we ever saw, so we thought it might be his mom. We'd like to think it was.

●●●●●●●

It was bizarre, it really was. It was nothing I would ever want to experience again. I'm glad nothing followed us!

I cried about it because I was so scared. When my husband would go teach at the college at night, I would sit in one spot and I would keep looking around. I was so scared. I did not like it. It was not a fun thing!

M. P. /J. P. July 30, 2001

8. WALKING DOWN THE ALLEY ROW

My father-in-law, whenever he was younger...probably in the 1950's... saw his friend walking down the alley row.

In them days, when you used to go to the toilet, you just "go" outside. He was [going] at the alley and [when he saw] his friend walk by he yelled at him, "Hey, what's the matter with you, aren't you gonna talk to me?"

[His friend] didn't answer him. He looked kind of dazed and just kept right on walking.

The next morning [my father-in-law] was still mad at him and was gonna ask him what his problem was. He was gonna go to his house, when he read in the news that [his friend] had died in a car wreck the night before...right at the same time he saw him [walking down] the alley!

Anonymous source. March 2001

9. AN OLD BLUE TRUCK

1993

This happened twice to me.

It was pretty late one night and I was driving my girlfriend back [to Starkville]. I dropped her off and I was going down this one old road, the one [that parallels] the highway. There are a lot of trees there, and a lot of old abandoned vehicles too. Anyway, I was on the road by myself. That road was really, really bad...full of potholes...so I was going pretty slowly. I looked in my rear view mirror and there were some headlights behind me. These lights kept getting closer and closer, [but] I couldn't really make out anything of the car. I just kept driving and when I got to the stop sign...the lights were gone! He could've pulled off somewhere I guess, but I would have seen him. He was right behind me, about twelve feet and catching up.

The second time, it was really dark and I was going down that same road. Those lights were there again...and speeding up. This vehicle pulled around me and I got a glimpse of it. It was an old blue truck, possibly from the 40's or 50's. What was really bizarre is when it passed me it was going really smooth, just gliding by. The road was kind of narrow and there's a bridge there. He would've had to go off into the grass to pass me, but it was going real smooth.

As it pulled in front of me, I could see in the truck's rear window...and [there was] no one driving! It went about a hundred feet and just faded away, it was no longer there!

Later, [my girlfriend's] mother told me there was a truck that once went off that old bridge. A couple of kids, two teenagers, died in the accident.

I didn't go on that road again!

R. C. March 10, 2002

10. SUPER BEE

I had this Dodge "Super Bee," that I bought new in '69 and got rid of in '71. I was late for school one morning and I was going down the street when I heard this voice yell, "STOP!"

I slammed on the brakes and this little kid ran out between two cars. I [probably] would've killed him, I was moving pretty good.

I looked in the rear view mirror and saw somebody sitting in the back seat. I couldn't see any facial features, just this silhouette. When I turned around to look, there was nobody there!

That happened to me two or three different times.

I was going down the highway one night and I heard this voice tell me, "TURN!" So I turned and this car came out of nowhere with no lights on. It pulled right out in front of me and [because I turned when I did] I missed him.

I was almost hit by a train once, and one time a deer jumped in front of [my car]. Something just told me to "STOP!"...And I slammed on the brakes. I would see him in the rear view mirror, but when I turned around and looked in the seat, he wasn't there.

I nicknamed him "George," but I actually think it was my guardian angel. I don't know for sure.

H. F. April 13, 2002

11. OUR HOUSE ON SECOND STREET

I believe our house on Second Street, the house we lived in for eighteen years, had spirits in it. I really believe that, because so many strange things happened. They were non-threatening. In fact, I always felt protected. I loved the house from the minute I walked into it.

●●●●●●●

We started hearing footsteps no more than a month after moving in. They became so commonplace that I didn't pay attention to them too much. But once, when I was there by myself, [I thought] I heard [my son] coming down the stairs. I went to the stairs and yelled, "T__?" before I remembered he was in California!

The footsteps always stopped at that turn coming down the stairs. They always stopped there.

One time my oldest daughter and son-in-law, when they were down visiting [from Pueblo], slept on the third floor. My daughter said they heard a roomer *(tenant)* we had at that time come in and go to his room *(also on the third floor)*. Then they heard other footsteps coming up the stairs and come right to their door and stop. My son-in-law would never sleep on the third floor again!

●●●●●●●

I've sat in the "blue room" and watched the doorknob turn that went out to the sun porch. I don't know how it turned or what caused it. It would turn and the door would open.

●●●●●●●

I never heard anyone [else] say anything, but my

[oldest daughter] did. One night she came and got in bed with me and said she was scared. She had started to go into her room, to get ready for bed, when a voice said, "What are you doing in here?" So, she ran in and crawled into bed with me!

●●●●●●●

[My youngest daughter] used to see "shadows." Twice, when she saw "dark" shadows in her room, her dad had an accident either on his way, or coming back, from work. And once she saw a "white" shadow. She had no fear of that one, but the dark shadows scared her. It seemed like something bad always happened when she saw them.

●●●●●●●

One night [my husband] was in Longmont, with his mother, and I felt him sit down on his side of the bed. I thought it was him. It woke me up and I reached over and turned on the night-light. I was going to ask him, "When did you get in?" You know, that sort of thing. But, when I looked there was no one there. It was so distinct. Someone sat on the side of the bed, but there was no one. So, I just turned off the light and went back to sleep!

●●●●●●●

I felt no fear in that house at all! And yet, I'm sure there were spirits in it. Once in the library, a hand was put on my shoulder, like reassurance. It was so nice.

I've never been in another house where I felt spirits, just that one. But I'm positive that they were there.

Built around 1900, the house, a three-story Victorian, was originally owned by a prosperous Trinidad businessman. It has passed through a number of different owners over the years and is now being used as a Bed and Breakfast.

I. S. August 4, 2001

12. COUSIN IRVIN

1957

Irvin was dad's cousin...I think a first cousin. He was a big tall man. I guess he was homely, but to me he wasn't because he was so nice. He always called me "Jimmy." I don't know why, but he did.

Irvin loved to fish. I used to go with him and just sit on the bank and watch him. And he whistled all the time he was fishing.

Anyway, he moved back to Arkansas, when his health started going bad on him.

When we lived on Tillotson Street, up by the college in Trinidad, I woke up one night and felt like someone was watching me. I sat up and Irvin was standing at the foot of my bed. He was just watching me, kind of half-smiling the way he used to. I thought I was dreaming at first, so I blinked a few times and lay back down. He was still there. So I sat up again, and I knew I was awake. He just stood there for...oh, not too long really...and then he just started fading away! I lay back down and went to sleep.

The next morning I went downstairs and told mamma what I had seen. And she said, "When we hear anything about Irvin, he'll either be really sick...or dead."

Well...I forgot about it. I just put it from my mind and forgot it.

That summer Irvin's sister, Alice, came to visit us with her daughter. And mamma said, "Alice, how is Irvin?"

She looked at mamma real funny and said, "Well, Louise, he's dead."

Mamma [then asked me], "Do you remember what happened?"

And I said, "No."

She said, "Remember when you thought you saw him?"

I said, "Well, yes." And of course I had seen him.

She asked Alice, "When did he die?" And I think Alice said in February of that year. Mamma went and got a calendar out of the kitchen, and she had marked down the morning I told her about the dream...or whatever it was. It was the same date that he had died.

I'm sure; when I saw him he was a spirit. I really believe that. He always liked me and I think, like mamma said, he just came to see me.

I. S. August 4, 2001

Torn down in the 1960's, the house once stood in the general vicinity of the Trinidad State Junior College bookstore.

13. THE OLD SCOUT

As a kid growing up in Trinidad, one of my all-time favorite ghost stories centered on the larger-than-life statue of Christopher "Kit" Carson, located next to the old bandstand in Kit Carson Park.

It was said...usually in a hushed whisper...you never, NEVER, wanted to enter the park after midnight, stand before the monument, and look Kit directly in the eye. If you were foolish enough to do so, the old scout and his horse would leap from their pedestal and chase you around town until morning!

It was also rumored that on particularly cold evenings, when there was no one around the park to chase, old Kit, looking for something to do, would ride to the nearest tavern. Once there, he'd sit by the fire, have a drink or two, or three or four, and swap lies with the locals!

Occasionally, after having a few too many, Kit would lose track of time and end up galloping wildly back to the park before sunrise. This helps to explain why every now and then you will find the old frontiersman, sitting stoically atop his faithful steed...with a beer can in his outstretched hand!

D. S. 2002

Said to be "one of the finest equestrian statues west of the Mississippi," The Kit Carson monument was sculpted in 1911-13 by New York artist Augustus Lukeman.

14. OLD JOE

Early 1980's

"Old Joe," that's what they called him.

In the restaurant's kitchen there's a little, tiny stairwell that goes to the basement...I used to hate to go to that basement when I was working there as a cook...when it was called the *"Beef & Brew."* They kept the potatoes in a niche where the wall was broken out down there, and they used it like a wine cellar and storage area. It made a good potato bin because it was nice and cool, but it just felt AWFUL in there! It wasn't like somebody was watching you. It was like somebody was crawling up your back. The hair's standing up on my neck now just thinking about it!

While I was working there, there was a robbery. We closed up around nine-thirty, ten o'clock, and everyone was out of there. When I went back to work the next day, some [people] came in and said they had seen a man in a white suit chasing two guys out the back door...which was a sliding glass door. And that this same person, this man, actually stopped at the back door, watched as these two guys ran away, then went back in.

He was wearing a white suit, a white fedora, completely in white. White shoes, everything, the whole bit.

They asked my boss if he was in [the restaurant], or if somebody was in there that night?

And he said, "No, we were closed and locked up."

The front door was open and the back was wide open. The stereo, located in the bar, was down off the shelf; nothing else had really been touched.

The people that had the restaurant before claimed that this person, this "Old Joe," had some connection to their family.

They say he watches over that place.

C. B. B. March 10, 2001

15. PICKETWIRE

We just had the restaurant [on Pine Street] for about nine months in 1984. We called it the *"Picketwire."* It later became another restaurant, but I don't remember the name.

Someone told me a story...one of my customers came in and talked to me. She said, kind of in a laughing way, "Have you had any encounters?"

I said "No." [Then] she told me about a waitress that had worked there another time...I don't know when.

The story was that the waitress was busy and was going through the front dining room. All of a sudden she noticed this woman sitting at a table, and she had "period" clothes on. You know, like in the 1800"s or something. The waitress thought, "Oh, I wonder if she's going to a play, or is in a play?" That was her thought.

She served her other customers, and then went back to this table to take the lady's order. And there wasn't anybody there! She asked somebody else in the room what happened to this lady, and nobody else had seen her.

Then there was another story about a family that came for dinner, a whole family of people here in town. They had finished eating, when somebody in their party asked who the woman was that came and sat down at their table...and then wasn't there! It sounded like the same woman the waitress had seen.

We heard repeated stories about people having seen or heard ghosts in the building *(see story #13)*. We never really saw anything. I remember...and I don't know if it was just suggestion, or what...but when I was in the basement a couple of times, doing some work in this little office down there, I felt like there was somebody watching me, or standing behind me. I wouldn't go down there anymore. It was just a real strong sense, and I didn't like it. I didn't feel that anywhere else in the building.

J. H. April 2001

16. A PHANTOM NUN

Built around 1889, Mount San Rafael Hospital was a massive, three-story stone structure that served all of Trinidad and Las Animas County for nearly one hundred years. It was replaced by a newer facility in the 1970's and was subsequently torn down in 1985-86.

Over the years, a number of strange tales have been told about old San Rafael, of which there is very little information today. One particular legend concerned a ghost that haunted the hospitals first and second floors.

Witnessed by both staff and patients alike, it was described as a phantom nun running through the hallways with a crying baby in her arms! This curious sight was supposedly reenacted once a year on a specific date, which, frustratingly, no one seems to remember.

I have also heard rumors of mysterious sounds and unexplained lights seen in the vicinity of the long departed building. These reports however are even more vague than the nun story.

D. S. 2002

GHOSTS OF THE "BACA/BLOOM"

Affectionately known by long-time residents as the "Baca/Bloom," the Trinidad History Museum was established in 1961 and is currently operated by History Colorado. Covering an entire block of East Main Street, the complex consists of the Santa Fe Trail Museum, the Baca House, the Bloom Mansion, and, according to some, a handful of restless spirits.

Built in 1870, the Baca House is said to be one of the oldest standing residents in Trinidad. Originally owned by local merchant John S. Hough, the two-story adobe structure was sold to rancher Don Felipe Baca (1829-1874) in 1873 for $7,000, furniture and all. It remained in the Baca family until 1931.

The Bloom Mansion, located just east of the Baca House, is a three-story Victorian built in 1882. Said to be one of the only remaining examples of "Second Empire architecture" in Colorado, it was the home of cattle rancher Frank G. Bloom

17. "KNOCK OFF THAT NOISE!"

My mom, you could say, had two different families. She had three children in `46, `48, and `50, and another set of children born in `61 and `63.

I was always with my sister, [she] was more of a mother figure. She was twelve years older and I was pretty much with her all the time.

I remember as a kid, she took me to Bloom Mansion. We were going through the mansion [and] walked up the stairs from the first floor to the second floor. I was standing just at the top of the stairs, kind of peeking around the door looking into the bedroom. The room was arranged as an office, and there was one of those old [roll-top] desks in the corner on the far side of the room. And there's an office chair...the old wooden style with a spring on the bottom that would rock...and this chair moved! It pulled forward, [or] sat forward.

I grabbed my sister by the pants and I was jerking on her legs. I whispered, "Hey, who is that over there?"

She said, "Who is what over where?"

I said, "That man over there!"

She said, "The man over where?"

"The man in the room over there, sitting at the desk!"

She told me, "I don't see anything over there, you're just seeing things." Then she asked, "What's he look like?"

"I told her, "He's got white hair and a beard."

She said, "Nah, I don't see anyone over there."

"Oh. Okay, whatever."

So, we went on with the tour.

The ghost was said to resemble the mansion's former owner Frank G. Bloom (1843-1931).

Some thirty-ish years later, I'm working at the [Bloom Mansion]. I went in the mornings to open up, you had to clean the house and make sure that everything is in its right place.

I was vacuuming the living room, or music room, on the left when you walk in the main door. The vacuum cleaner was plugged in to a socket in the dining room and my back is to that door. I hear this noise, "LA, LAA, LAAA!" Like a kid...and my little brother used to do this...trying to match the pitch of the vacuum cleaner, or override the sound, seeing if he could get louder than that. And I hear from behind me, "Knock off that noise!" Of course, I'm alone in the house. I turned around and there's nobody there.

The sound that I thought was a little boy stopped and I continued to vacuum. I felt a tap on my shoulder, and in my right ear I hear, "I TOLD YOU TO KNOCK OFF THAT NOISE!" I turned around, put my hands on my hips, and I told him. "I'll stop when I'm finished, thank you!"

He *(Frank Bloom?)* never bothered me again, as far as that goes.

The "little boy" is thought to be Frank Bloom Jr., who died of typhoid in 1889.

●●●●●●●

Another time I was doing a thorough cleaning and I decided to check out the basement and the third floor. "Curiosity killed the cat." I always wanted to and I was going to do it!

I went downstairs into the basement and there's a pool in the floor, like a Roman bath type of thing. There's also a pit there and a furnace next to it. There's just this feeling of oppressiveness, very, very thick air, and it's just kind of in a concentrated area right there. It's just in one specific area that you could feel it. So, I go upstairs, and it (*the strange feeling*) penetrated through the house. Up through the middle, kind of where the hallway is, all the way up past the third floor. It's just a very eerie feeling. [There's] nothing specific that I can tell about what it is, it's just that it's there. It's almost like a void, or vortex. Very, very weird and very, very heavy. Just kind of hair-raising I guess.

●●●●●●●

I don't know if I ever saw [Frank Junior]. I always heard him, usually on the main floor between the stairs and the wall that separated the dinning room and the hallway from the stairwell. I could hear a ball, like if you were sitting with your back against the wall and you took a ball and you did a double-bounce...throwing it against the floor, hit the wall, and back to you. That type of thing.

Upstairs on the second floor, I'd hear giggles and stuff like that. On occasion, in the back bedroom...the daughter's bedroom...there's some activity there. I've been told that people have seen a chair move in there.

C. B. B. March 10, 2001.

18. CURTAINS

Our shift [at the police department] used to end about two o'clock in the morning. [The old courthouse] was a well-lighted place and it was no trouble walking down the stairs to your car. But you always got that funny, eerie feeling that something was watching you from those top windows of the Baca House, facing west. A couple of times...I know that those little curtains were closed, but one of them would be open. I knew I wasn't tired and I knew it wasn't my imagination.

There were some times, certain times of the year like in March, or the first part of October; the alarm would go off in the Bloom Mansion. But none of the officers wanted to go! They said in the back part *(between the Baca House and the Bloom Mansion)* there was an old wagon there. You could see...I hate to use the word "spirit"...this "thing" kind of "walking" near the wagon. It would never look at you, it would just walk around. I think whatever was there used to go to the Bloom house. It would sit and relax and rock in the chair!

We used to laugh and say, "The ghost set off the alarm again in the Bloom." Well, I really think there was a ghost there, and I really think there still is. The officers themselves, they would tell me stories about one time they had to go in [the Bloom]. When an officer has to check an alarm they never turn on the lights, they have to walk it in the dark. This one particular officer told me that when he was shining his [flash] light, it hit a mirror and he saw his light come back. But, standing between him and the mirror there was this other "person!" The officer just left, he said everything was okay and that was it! After that they used to make the museum curator *(director)* go with them to check the place, to make sure the doors and windows were secure. They didn't want to go in there anymore. Whatever was in there, it didn't do anything to hurt them, it was just the idea that they weren't by themselves in there.

A couple of times it had started to snow and I was walking to my car. I would get this ugly feeling like someone was watching me. A buddy was cleaning [the ice] off my windshield and was doing my side windows. I sat in the car and I looked up. Sure enough, those curtains were open on the Baca House!

K. T. July 21, 2001.

19. A BLOOD SPOT ON THE FLOOR

The Baca House always seemed to be "clean" *(spiritually)* to me. I know that there was some pretty nasty things that happened in that house. There was a murder in the 40's in there and stuff like that. I know that some people say they've seen things and a few say they've seen a blood spot on the floor. And yeah, it's there.

There is a spot on the floor where at certain times of the day, during certain times of the year, when the light is just right, you can see a saturation on the floor. It's a hardwood floor, so there is somewhat of a stain there. If you know where it's at you can probably spot it, but the lighting's got to be right to tell.

That house has always been comfortable. I have never felt any "energy" in there other than good energy.

C. B. B. March 10, 2001

20. SILHOUETTE

It wasn't the Bloom Mansion so much for me; it was always the Baca House.

At night you would see shadows, like there were people in there. It was always in the upstairs window.

We used to [ignore] it because the alarm system never went off. And that place had alarms everywhere! You would justify in your mind, "Well, maybe they have a mannequin up there, or something."

But I've seen that silhouette in the Baca House a couple of times.

Former Trinidad Police officer, 2002

According to museum staff, mannequins have never been used in any of the Baca House displays.

21. POSADA

It was a few years ago. We were working over at the Baca House during the *Posada*, the procession at Christmas time where Mary and Joseph go around to all the houses [seeking shelter]. We were in the house and there weren't any lights on, or candles, or anything. It was cold, and dark, and windy. We were just standing by the front door and we could hear what sounded like someone walking across the floor upstairs...more than once.

It sounded like someone walking, not just a creak. You know, how a floor can creak, but it was an actual walk.

Anonymous source, 2002

22. LITTLE NAME TAGS

While gathering material for this section, I had the good fortune to sit and talk with Paula Manini, Director of the Trinidad History Museum since 1991. During our conversation, I asked how she felt about the ghostly rumors, and other oft-told tales, surrounding the Baca/Bloom.

Well, there haven't been a lot of stories, but there are definitely a few, especially from the people who work here as tour guides. They swear they've had experiences in the house *(Bloom Mansion)* with ghosts. I've never experienced it myself and neither has Manuel, who has worked here since 1966.

I've heard people say that they've walked into the Bloom study and a chair would be rocking. Another person said they saw a shadow, the outline of a figure with a cowboy hat. They assumed that it was Frank Bloom, although he probably wouldn't be wearing a hat inside! A house cleaner who worked here had her little baby in a backpack, or carrier. She said the baby would always get really animated, like when there was another kid around. The Mother always had this sense that her baby was interacting with another child.

And then a friend of mine who visited is sensitive to psychic phenomena, or whatever. She would say, and we've had a couple of different people say this, "I feel the presence of a child in there."

It was funny when Mary Sue Mangino wrote the play for the Halloween program we did *(October, 1999)*. When Mary Sue and I were around asking questions of the tour guides, they said, "Oh no, I'm afraid of ghosts. I just go straight in there and turn off the alarm. I don't look around, I don't look to the side, I just stare straight ahead!" Everybody starts getting a little freaky once you start talking about it.

Everybody, even visitors, if they feel anything are more likely, much more likely, to ask if the Bloom is haunted and not the Baca House. I think part of that might be that we had a long period when we were having a hard time getting contractors to work on the Bloom, and the house was looking a bit shabby. Paint was peeling off and it was kind of decrepit looking, so it had a creepy feeling. And when you go inside it's dark. It has heavy, dark wallpaper, heavy curtains, so it lends itself more to hauntings. It's an old Victorian, so people assume that it's haunted.

And then, I don't know how long I had been working at the museum, but we had a school group here. We were around the Bloom and they were kind of whispering and pointing at the fence. I asked, "What are you guys talking about?"

"Is it true that the Bloom family are buried over there?" And they pointed at the rose bushes along the wall.

I said, "No they're buried in the cemetery! Why do you think that?"

"Well, they've got those little name tags!"

They were identification tags naming the people who have donated various kinds of antique roses to our garden. Somehow just seeing these I.D. tags, that are maybe three or four inches wide, was enough for them to think they were graves.

I was telling Manuel, who has worked here for so long, about that and he said, "Oh yeah, every once in a while someone comes in and says that. And not just kids, but a couple of adults, old timers in Trinidad, say that too."

I only remember one tour guide saying anything about the Baca House, even though there was an actual murder that took place in the house *(September 15, 1945)*. A man murdered his wife upstairs when it was a boarding house. This one tour guide would say, "When the lighting is just right you can see a pool of blood on the floor *(see story #20)*."

No one else, visitors or staff, have ever said, "I feel something in this house," or "This house is creepy." It's bright and cheery, with those white washed adobe walls.

I've never seen anything. If you let your imagination go and start listening to all these things people say, you can walk in there and kind of "psyche" yourself out.

I believe in ghosts and think it would be cool to see one. But I never have.

P. M. April 26, 2001

PART TWO:
COUNTY GHOSTS.
SNEED 2002

23. A LITTLE GIRL ALL DRESSED IN WHITE

[Our] ranch, or farm...or whatever you want to call it...used to be near Alfalfa, about thirty miles from Trinidad. And what we lived in was called the Horseshoe Ranch, because the ditch went around *(horseshoe shape)* and the house sat kind of in the middle.

My sister and I were playing in the house...either playing or fighting, I can't recall. Anyway, I ran out of the house and around this ditch there were a bunch of bushes. And I ran between the bushes. I don't know, maybe I was small, so I may have wanted to hide. But, as I looked out across...the ditch ran this way and there was a fence here *(opposite the ditch)*...I saw this little girl all dressed in white. When she bent down to go under the gate, the fence, she just disappeared. And I had the most awesome feeling.

It was really wonderful to see this, because it was just a little girl all dressed in white and I wanted to go there *(to the fence)* and see where she had gone.

Later, mamma said she was from Australia *(?)*, the little girl. So we took our shovels, 'cause mom and dad said Australia was straight across...down from us...[and] we started digging! We were going to Australia to find the little girl!

She had long...it must have been light hair... because everything looked white. And she was wearing a white, long dress. And, you know, 'cause it was a ways [away]; you couldn't see a face or anything. All you could see was her running away. It was really a fantastic feeling that I got from seeing her.

An interesting question was asked yesterday, when I was telling this story [to some relatives]. She *(pointing to her sister)* was asking if it was close to where maybe there had been Indians or whatever...which the Santa Fe Trail did run right there by the house. She said it might have been a child who was killed or died when going across country in the covered wagons.

I can still see it, just like it happened then. It was in the late 30's, about 1936.

A. H. / C. V. May 17, 2001

First settled in 1864, Alfalfa was a small farming/ ranching community about 25 miles southeast of Trinidad. Named for the principal crop grown in the area, it was abandoned shortly after the end of World War II.

The original Santa Fe Trail, founded by William Becknell, went through the Alfalfa area in 1821. When the main route was relocated further west, over Raton Pass, freight wagons and cowboys driving cattle to market used the old road.

Little or no trace of Alfalfa remains today.

24. THE CRYING OF THE INDIANS

An aunt, which was an aunt to my father...to our father...used to tell us that the Cherokee Indians was chased west from the east coast of the Carolina's. Treaty after treaty was broken. They were promised this land, that land, and the other land. Way back, towards the east coast, there was buffalo, so many that they could just stampede for days on end. But as they came west, the white man had killed all the buffaloes.

And she said, "Honey, the prairies were white with bones, white with bones."

You've read about the "Trail of Tears?" I really feel that was what she was referring to. Because she said that there in the Red Rocks area...across the river from where we lived, which was Alfalfa...if you listen carefully, on a still night, you can hear this crying. The crying of the Indians. She said it was just pitiful!

C. V. May 17, 2001

25. SHE COULD HEAR THEM, BUT THEY WEREN'T THERE

1930's

Where we lived was way down where the original Santa Fe Trail was *(near Alfalfa)*. The Indians were there first, of course, then the wagon trains would come through, and also, I think, the Pony Express. But, anyway, our grandmother would tell my mother that once in a while, when she was home alone in the evening...and we were all in adobe houses in those days, coal oil lamps and what have you...she could hear the Indians chasing down a covered wagon, or whatever it was. You know, they would make their "whooping" noise. And she said she could hear them, but they weren't there. She could just hear their ghosts, or whatever it was that was there, you know.

She could hear that every once in awhile. She says invariably when she was home alone...grandpa wasn't there [he was out] doing something...she'd hear that. The horses galloping and the Indians chasing the wagon train.

S. L. May 17, 2001

26. INDIAN GHOST

The story as told by Mr. Bransford is as follows: A short time ago Mr. Juan Vasquez, who resides half a mile west of Bransford's ranch, while digging a foundation for a house struck an old graveyard. The bones and skulls are nearly double the size of those of the present day. The Pueblo Indians and Mexicans have no record of any graveyard in that vicinity and say that it must be very ancient or they would know something about it. The bones on being exposed to the air crumbled to dust, and it is next to impossible to obtain one in entire. Several bones have been sent to Dr. Beshoar of Trinidad, who says they average much larger than those of any man living today, and must be the remains of a race of giants. And now comes

THE GHOST.

On the evening of the day on which the grave yard was "struck," the son of Mr. Bransford, a young man, twenty years of age, distinctly saw standing in the doorway, an apparition of an Indian Chief, very large, and having a white face. The figure was dressed in a white costume different from anything he had ever seen. It beckoned him to advance, but he turned in affright, to wake a friend sleeping in the same apartment, and upon looking again the goblin had vanished. The same night a Mexican girl residing two miles up the creek saw and describes the same apparition. Mr. Bransford says that knocks are heard at all hours of the night upon his door and roof, and that his dogs, which are ordinarily very vicious, appear to take no notice of the disturbance.

ANOTHER MYSTERY.

In connection with the above, and a nut for spiritualists to crack, is the following: In the evening and while we were sitting around the fire place, two sticks of wood, which were burning at the time, began to dance, and in a few moments one of them suddenly went up the chimney and landed thirty yards from the house, where we found it still burning. It made no explosion and left no smell of Sulphur or other combustible. There are certainly some things difficult of explanation in that neighborhood, and to which I would call the attention of the scientific party now visiting our territory. Another mystery, and unexplainable to all who have ever yet visited the premises is the

DEVIL'S CHMNEY.

On the garden of Mr. Bransford are two piles or mounds of stone. Through one of these mounds issue constantly two small columns of smoke, apparently caused by the burning of wood. The ground for fifty feet in the neighborhood sounds hollow, and gives one the feeling as if walking on the deck of a ship. While visiting there the proprietor allowed us to dig through the mounds for the purpose of investigating the cause of the smoke. We dug down about ten feet but did not clear up the mystery. We found, however at that depth a specimen of *malpais*, which at some remote age has been used by Indians for grinding grain.

The Rocky Mountain News. December 20, 1870. Reprinted with the permission of the Rocky Mountain News.

The Bransford Ranch was located near Barela, a small farming village 20 miles southeast of Trinidad.

27. A STRANGE PIECE OF COUNTRY

These situations started many years ago, when my wife and I were dating. I was [living] in Trinidad and she was [living] in Tyrone. One evening we were out at Tyrone, it was already dark, about eleven o'clock at night, and the whole area...the whole countryside where her mom and dad's house was...just turned like daylight. And I mean this was in the middle of the night! It wasn't lightning, or floodlights, or anything of that sort. It just turned like daylight, you could see from horizon to horizon. I don't know how long it lasted, but it was for a period of time. Needless to say, it frightened both of us!

That was just one instance.

●●●●●●●

After we were married, we were down [near Tyrone] and we were camping in our trailer. We went down to antelope hunt. We parked the trailer out on the prairie, and in the middle of the night our trailer started rocking violently. I assumed it was a cow, you know, rubbing on the trailer and just rocking it. I got up but couldn't see anything, and then there was something working on the door, like it wanted to open the door. Of course, again, we were very frightened. But nothing came in.

We got out and couldn't see any tracks anywhere. There were no cows around; there were no people around. There was nothing. The next morning we got up to check the trailer to see if we could see any tracks, or if somebody was playing a joke on us, anything of that sort. We thought maybe a raccoon tried to open the door or something. There were no tracks anywhere.

Have you driven those prairie roads down there? The dust flies and the backside of your trailer and the backside of your truck, everything, is just full of dust. There was nothing that indicated a cow was there. Something had to be there, but who knows what!

●●●●●●●

I think the third [incident] that really surprised us, was when we were going in there real late at night. We used to leave Denver and go down after work. There were bright lights ahead of us, as though something was in the road. You would imagine it was a deer, or something of that sort. I'm an outdoorsman, and I always carry a powerful spotlight. I turned on the spotlight and there was absolutely nothing there! We'd turn the spotlight back out, drive a little ways down the road, and the same thing would happen. These big old eyes, they looked like eyes, right in the middle of the road! We'd stop, turn the spotlight on, and again there was nothing there.

This was witnessed by more than just me, my wife and kids and others. It kind of startled us because I always assumed it was a cow or deer, [maybe] a fox or coyote, 'cause we see them out there all the time. When you see eyes in the road, typically that's what it is. But when you stop and you put those big spotlights on... they're really powerful and light up the whole countryside...and there's nothing there, you kind of wonder what it was.

●●●●●●●

My son and his fiancée went down there on motorcycles one time. This would have to be the early to mid-90's. They stopped at the ranch to visit with my brother-in-law and spend the night with him. They wanted to go out on the prairie that night to see the stars and, you know, being from Denver, experience the outdoors. He wouldn't let them go.

He told us a lot of things, and is not an individual that would stretch things too much. He's a rancher and he just said, "There are things out there that you guys don't know about, but they're here. Tomorrow you can see all you want, but not at night."

It's a strange piece of country out there!

C. A. July 22, 2001

Located 30 miles northeast of Trinidad, Tyrone was a small farming village and a station on the Atchison, Topeka &

28. NOTHING TO HURT A PERSON

We moved up here from Texas in `46. Our farm is [just a few miles] east of Trinidad, and we have land on both sides of the highway and both sides of the [Purgatoire] river.

I don't know how old [our first house] is. Part of it is adobe, part of it is frame, and part of it is cinder block. I think the adobe part could be a hundred years old and, you know, they started adding on. Anyway, we lived there...the whole family lived there...until we built another house [near the old one].

I really can't remember anything strange happening until we moved out of that old house. My dad passed away in `94, and things seemed to start happening then.

•••••••

My nephew had different jobs and would stay here [on the farm] for a while then move off. He decided that he wanted to stay in that old house. He and a buddy were staying in there and they would hear doors open and close. They would put their money and watches and stuff by their bed on a little table. In the morning it wasn't there, it was moved to a different place.

One night they heard something outside. They went out and walked around the house to see if they could see anything. My nephew was going one way and his friend was going the other way. [My nephew] said he could hear footsteps right behind him. He thought it was his buddy, so he turned around and there was no one there. This was in the middle of the night, it's dark out there, and it's kind of scary!

Occasionally he would feel a breeze, like someone was walking in front of him. One time, he walked into the kitchen and saw a shadow...a dark shadow of a person. He said it disappeared, [and] that really shook him up!

Footsteps, doors closing and stuff, went on as long as he stayed there.

●●●●●●●

[My nephew] eventually moved off. Then, strange things started in our new house! A dish would fall. We would hear someone walking. One time I was by myself and I felt somebody sit down on the bed. You would feel the bed go down and there was no one there.

My sister had a lot of experiences over in her house too. She just lives about a hundred yards from our house.

One night there was a red light outside her back window. She said it just stayed there for a little bit. There was no one out there, but that light was there.

One time, she got up in the morning and...her table is always clean...there was a box of crackers that she had never seen before, sitting on that table partly eaten. You know, it looked like somebody was sitting there eating those things.

Just the other day, we were over at her house. We were

sitting at the table talking. The table is in her dining room and the kitchen is right connected. All of a sudden a knife flew out of the kitchen, went across the room and landed on the floor! She [kept all] her knives in a compartment.

Every now and then the lights would go on and off over [in the old house]. One night, maybe about a year ago, I saw a light on over there. No one lives there anymore, and the power has to be turned on at a separate breaker-box.

●●●●●●●

One time, [my wife] was in the house by herself...the new house, and daddy had passed away already...when all of a sudden she saw daddy standing there! She described him...he used to wear those bib-overalls and stuff like that...and she said he was standing there with his overalls on. She saw him for just a second.

She came running out to try and find me, but I was out in the yard a long ways away.

I don't know. It was nothing to hurt a person, but it was just weird things happening. Things we can't explain.

T. M. /E.V. February 11, 2002

29. DUST

1950

It was just an odd little thing that happened.

Us kids, we used to go to Aguilar from Lynn to ride the horses. They didn't have the roads paved then, you know, it was just dirt. We used to go there and ride the horses like crazy down those dirt roads!

Well, this car went around us and kicked up a lot of dust. It was probably, for that time, a fairly new car. A Buick or Mercury, something like that. But floating over the top of this car [in the dust] was a silhouette, a perfect silhouette of this old square back, rumble seat-type car! And there were two people in there, a man and a woman, and the woman had on a hat. It was just as plain as day! As the dust faded, so did the silhouette. It just went away.

I hollered at the others, "Did you see that!?"

"See what? See what?"

By that time it was already gone. But it was sure plain, just as plain as if somebody had drew it up over that other car.

For a long time I wouldn't say anything, because I thought people would think I was nuts. It actually happened! I can still see that in my mind today. I don't know what it was, it was just... interesting.

S. C. August 6, 2001

Lynn was a tiny railroad stop about two miles north of Aguilar.

30. GHOST LIGHTS

Early 1900's

Did you ever hear of the "ghost lights?" Mother talked about them all the time. She used to see them when she was staying in her grandmother's "dugout" on the flats, just northeast of Aguilar.

Have you ever been in a dugout? They were just one big room. They had a stove, of course, no refrigerator...they didn't have refrigerators then. They had chests of drawers, built-in shelves and a dirt floor. That was all.

Mamma went out and stayed with grandma a lot when she was a kid. She said that one night, she and grandma were out watching the prairie, and they saw car lights coming...'cause it was flat and you could see a long way. At least they thought it was a car. It came down the road and made the curve to turn into the farm. It just got so close to the house, and then it stopped and started backing up. It backed up the same way and then just went out, it disappeared.

It was just the lights. It might have been "heat lightning," I don't know. Scientists have a lot of different theories, but mom said it looked just like car lights.

Mamma said there was no sound, no sound like a car. Of course in those days, you know, those old Model T's rattled. She said there was no sound at all. It went right down the road the way a car would go.

A lot of people called them the ghost lights. There used to be a lot of ghost lights out there along this trail they said the Indians used to take, and where a bunch of them were killed. Up until dad and mom passed away, they would call them ghost lights. Dad would call them "Jack-o-lanterns" too, but mom called them ghost lights, because they went right along that trail where the Indians had been pushed along and died.

Isn't that something?

I. S. December 3, 2001

31. HAND-ME-DOWNS

2000

Well, when we lived out on a farm [near Hoehne], it was about two or three months before we were going to move back to New England. My husband and I would always fall asleep on the couch watching TV. He woke up and he looked over at the doorway that goes down the hall. He thought our daughter was standing in the hallway. He said, "Okay J____, go back to bed." He closed his eyes back again, and he's thinking, "Wait a minute, she was dressed!"

So he looked back over there again, and to make sure he wasn't dreaming he looked at the clock, and then he looked at the figure. It was a little boy. He was probably my daughter's age, about eight or nine. He had pants that were rolled up, old cowboy boots, and a plaid shirt with rolled up sleeves. It was like...hand-me-downs stuff. I don't know if he had a hat on, but he had a dirty face and dark hair. [My husband] just looked at it for a couple of seconds, it turned and it disappeared, just vanished. He woke me up going, "M____, M____! There's something in the doorway and it wasn't J____!"

We lived there for almost a year and a half. We never had any kind of "thing" until a couple of months before we were leaving. Maybe "he" was kind of upset that we were leaving. Maybe he felt at home that we were there.   I don't know.   It just wanted to make its presence known, that somebody was there.

Hoehne is a small farming village about 10 miles northeast of Trinidad.

M. P. July 30, 2001

32. UNCLE BERNABE

1917

Uncle Bernabe was planning to attend a dance one Saturday night. He was interested in a lovely young girl, Querina *(his future wife)*, who would also be at the dance.

It was spring, and the headgates of the acequia *(irrigation ditch)* were open. Each daybreak, the water was closed off in some fields and reopened in others by hand-shoveling mounds of dirt to block and unblock the flow of water. Sugar beets, beans, corn, wheat, and the family's vegetable garden were planted and beginning to sprout.

The early morning chore of changing the water was partly Uncle Bernabe's and, knowing he would be returning from the dance by horseback very late, my grandfather forbade him to leave the farm *(northwest of Hoehne)* that Saturday night.

Grandpa always went to bed very early in the evening, and that night, as soon as he went to his room, Uncle Bernabe was off to the dance on his favorite horse, a "pinto." Uncle Bernabe was a charming, handsome man. He had a great sense of humor, told great stories, and loved people, so he had a grand time that night at the dance.

Leaving the dance after midnight, Uncle Bernabe was drowsy, but the pinto knew his way home. As they traveled, the night became increasingly stormy and lightning struck in the distance.

Slouched in the saddle, Uncle Bernabe's hair suddenly stood up on end. He sat up looking through the darkness but saw nothing. When he turned around, in the distance, he saw a bright moving light. As it came nearer, he saw that it was a fire, a burning ball of fire! It traveled quickly rolling along the surface of the fields behind him. As it came closer, he spurred his horse, trying to outrun the rolling flame, but it steadfastly followed the horse and man, neither gaining ground nor dropping behind. Uncle Bernabe said it rose and fell, just above the surface of the ground as it moved somewhere behind him. The blazing ball kept to its course for what seemed an eternity to my uncle. At last, as he was nearing the family farm, the glare began to fade and then finally disappeared into darkness.

Uncle Bernabe made it home safely that early Sunday morning. He said that the scare made him more aware of his life. Also, because of its role in this experience, he dearly loved his pinto. In fact, one of the things we most remember is his favorite statement that he was considering trading Aunt "Katie" (*Querina, whom he was married to for probably sixty years*) in exchange for a pinto!

Contributed by D. M. March 28, 2002

33. SHADOW

That house we lived in [near Valdez] belonged to Ringo's (*the local grocery/general store*) and on occasion we had something, a spirit I think, come up the basement stairs and go to the window in the bedroom. And you could see the shadow of this spirit, just standing there. It would stand there a little while, and then go back downstairs. It did it once or twice a month and nobody bothered it and it didn't bother anybody else.

We lived there twelve years and it happened at least once a month, sometimes [more]. It was about the 'same time every month. It was just like a shadow, that's all it was.

And the house we live in now, we still have [a spirit]. Whether it's the same one that followed us, or it's a different one, I don't know. But it does the same thing. It comes up from the basement and goes to the kitchen window, stands there for a few seconds and then goes back to the basement. But it also plays tricks on me, this one. It turns the lights off. And sometimes I think it's laughing, because I can sit there for three hours and I'm fine. The minute I'm all by myself it turns the lights off. I [call] it nasty things!

[The house] is next door to the one we lived in before. Whether we took him with us or it's a new one I don't know, but it's actions are the same. Except it turns the lights off and makes me aggravated!

N. B. March 28, 2001

Located one mile east of Segundo and 16 miles west of Trinidad, Valdez was a small coal camp established in the early 1900's.

34. PACINO'S

Mid 1970's

Valdez was a nice little mining camp and there were quite a few grocery stores, bars, and stuff like that. Pacino's [Bar] was an adobe structure that had been abandoned for quite a few years.

I think I was about fourteen. It was Halloween night and we (*family and friends*) went out right after dark and had gone down toward the L_____'s place. We were walking right in front of Pacino's. There was a big plate window...it was open of course...the window wasn't there. There was a door and another big plate window, a wall, and another section of the building that was really run down. There was a big storefront area and a door going to the back room. The front part was probably eighteen to twenty feet wide. On the other side of the doorway, there was this old coal stove and an old teapot sitting on top this stove.

We were going by there. Everybody was goofing around, and I'm watching this old store as we walk by. Off the stove comes floating up this knife! Of course, you know your imagination can get away from you, especially on Halloween night, so I don't know how much I really did see. This knife came out of that room, toward the wall. It almost went to the wall, then came back and was facing out the window. I'm turned around watching this, and it *(the knife)* is floating in the middle of the room. And then the teapot on the stove picks up and it tips over. I yelled at everybody, "RUN, D-----T, RUN!" And this knife just went "THUNK" and popped into the wall on the far end, between the window casing and the wall.

I went back the next day to look...there was no way I was going there at night...and there was a gash in the wall where the knife had stuck! There was nothing in there, the knife wasn't there, but the teapot was on the floor in the back.

That was kind of wild.

C. B. B. March 10, 2001

35. WHAT HAPPENED TO YOUR FRIENDS?

Summer, 1996

In a canyon not far from Trinidad, there sits the remains of a small Spanish settlement that dates back to the late 1800's. Now abandoned, it is today a cluster of adobe houses in various states of decay, a *Morada*, once used by local *Penitentes* as a gathering place during Holy week, and a small cemetery. *(The landowners have had a great deal of trouble with theft and vandalism over the years, so I do not wish to give the old settlement's exact location).*

As a kid, I was intrigued with this particular place and would have explored every building and read every headstone if given half a chance. Unfortunately, the old village was fenced and clearly marked "PRIVATE PROPERTY, " so I rarely ventured any farther than the road.

On my return to Trinidad...having lived in Denver for sixteen years...I happened across a newsletter that mentioned this particular settlement. In the article the writer stated that a small gap had been left in the fence, for those individuals who wished to "respectfully" visit the site. I drove up a few days later. Sure enough, there was an opening in the fence.

I wandered about the old cemetery..., which resembles the classic "boot hill" typified in most Western movies...for about thirty minutes or so. It was choked with weeds and cactus, and the headstones were scattered about in no particular order. One marker, the obvious victim of vandals, lay in pieces on the ground. For some reason, I was compelled to stop and put the stone back together.

As I finished my task, I noticed an old, silver-gray pickup truck coming down the road toward the settlement. Not knowing whom it was...and still not convinced I should be there...I walked down the hill to meet them. As I reached my own truck, they pulled up and parked next to me.

My unexpected guests turned out to be an old couple that had lived at the settlement prior to World War II. They just happened to be driving by, saw my truck, and were curious to see who I was and what I was doing.

We talked for about an hour and the old man gave me a short history of the community and it's former inhabitants. As we spoke, I couldn't help but notice that every now and then he would turn and look up at the cemetery. Finally, as we were all getting ready to leave, he asked, "Hey, what happened to your friends?"

I wasn't exactly sure what he meant, since I was the only one there at the time. When I told him that I was alone, he gave me a strange look and said, "When we were driving up, we saw you coming down the hill and there were two other people behind you."

"I saw them too!" said his wife, who had hardly spoken a word before now, "It was another man and a woman."

I must admit, I haven't been back there since that time, at least not by myself!

D. S. December, 2001

The Penitentes, also known as "The Brothers of Our Father Jesus," are affiliated with the Catholic Church and were organized to help the needy (the sick, the poor, widows, orphans, etc.) in isolated villages where "social services were nonexistent and few priests were available."

36. A LITTLE OLD MAN

1931

As a little girl I remember playing house with my friend. We lived up on a hill in North Fork (*Parras Plaza*) and we used to go up and eat and come down and play. A big rock used to be our table and the little weeds that were around were our vegetables.

We were playing there one morning and my mamma called us, so we went up to eat and we climbed that little hill. We lived on top, and down at the bottom we had our well and we had like a nook. So, we went to eat and then we came down. [My friend] went one way and I ran the other way, and we were going to meet by that little table by the ditch. As I came around the corner, there was a little old man sitting where I was supposed to be making my little vegetables. My girlfriend came and she looked at me, and I looked at her. It was a little man dressed, like my grandpa told me, "Could've been a hermit, could've been Saint Joseph." He had a cane and a long beard and he wore like a gunnysack, you know, like a...[monk's robes].

He went like that at me *(motioning to come closer)* and I thought, "No way! I'm going up the hill again!"

So [my friend] ran up one-way and I ran up the other way and went to my grandpa and his friend. My grandpa was, you know, *Penitente,* and we met him and he was doing something up on the hill with his shovel. We both ran and told him to go down and see what that little man wanted.

And my grandpa said, "What man?"

And I said "He's got a long beard and he goes like that *(motioning)* to me with his hand to go to him. He's got a long cane, and he's holding on to it like that *(tightly)*."

And [grandpa's] friend went this way [down the hill], and we followed him, and my grandpa went the other way and, it was just a matter of twenty minutes, and we didn't find nothing. So my grandpa looked at me, and I said, "Honest grandpa, I'm not lying."

And the other girl came and told him, "No, we saw him, it was a little man dressed in brown with a long beard."

And my grandpa went one way [around the hill] and his friend went down to the river, because an old man like that couldn't have gone very far in twenty minutes. Well, they never saw him. And so we kept on playing there!

1936

And then after that, my sister lived...we lived on top of the hill...and she lived [across] the arroyo. She was married and had kids, and her life was a little miserable, and we used to go visit her all the time.

So one day, I was running and had to go barefooted through the canal, to get from one side of the arroyo to the other, where the water runs through the ditch. So I used to take my shoes off and run through there and...I must have been about [15] years old...and I ran 'cause I saw the little old man sitting not too far from where I glanced up. And it was the same little old man!

I ran and told my sister, and she said, "Well let me look at him."

She had an incident when she was first married of a man like that. So she ran...up the arroyo...and he was just sitting there going like that (motioning) to us. And when I hollered at my sister, she ran over [to the little man] and he disappeared.

So that was the second time I saw him. And I told my sister about it and she said, "That's the same man that came to visit me when [we] lived in La Veta, in some canyon."

1928

My brother-in-law had been making props (*wooden support beams for the mines*), and about four feet of snow had fallen, and [my sister] had a cabin. And this little old man...and there were only three cabins, for the three workers...came and knocked on the door. My brother-in-law was a mean guy, you know, and he opened the door and said, "What do you want?"

And [the little man] says, "I would like to have a place to sleep and eat tonight."

And my sister went over there and she said, "What does

he want?"

And my brother-in-law...and this was all in Spanish...said, "He wants to eat and sleep here, but he can get the hell outta here, 'cause I haven't got anything like that for nobody!"

So my sister said, "Why don't you let him sleep, 'cause he looks like he's hungry."

And my brother-in-law said, "No!"

Well, the next morning they didn't find no steps going to the cabin, but there were footprints [going away from] there. [The little man] went around the corner to the next cabin. But he never got to the other cabin. Nobody ever saw anybody! And [the little man] was the same one I described to [my sister].

She claims that maybe God had sent somebody to "try" my brother-in-law to see if his heart would be kind to somebody, you know, because he wasn't kind to anybody.

H. J. March 28, 2001

37. TWO COMPANIONS

My grandpa, when my grandma died, my mom brought him back with us from Colorado Springs. He had [originally] come from New Mexico. He was raised with the son of an Indian Chief, in a pueblo of the Indians. After he got older, well, naturally he met my grandma somewhere, you know.

He was a *Penitente.* They used to come from what they called a *Morada,* a gathering [place] of the *Penitentes* on Wednesday, Thursday, Friday, and Saturday noon on Holy week *(Lent)*.

He used to tell us stories about one time that he was coming from the Morada, way up by where we lived *(North Fork)*. [The *Penitentes*] had to cross through the mountains and come and visit another *Morada*. One time, they sent him alone. They had what they called the *Hermano Mayor (Elder Brother)* and he told them what to do in that organization.

They told [grandpa] that he had to come and pay a visit to *Our Lady of Guadalupe* Church. I don't know whether he came with a cross or with a whip. He started off alone. Pretty soon he turned around and he had two companions with him. He never talked and they never said anything. They would motion...because he turned around and wanted to talk to them...to "Keep going, keep going."

And so he said [to us], "Coming around to where they left me off at the church, they disappeared."

He asked next day, you know, the *Hermano Mayor*, "Did you send somebody to watch me?"

[He] said, "No, that was supposed to be done by yourself."

[Grandpa] said, "But I had two companions!"

"Well, we didn't do it."

So, it had to be somebody maybe sent by God. They were strong believers in that.

H. J. September 1, 2001

38. EL JUDIO ERRANTE

1930's

We lived right there in North Fork. The house is falling down now. I'm trying to get it back so I can clean the yard and leave the two cabins that are there, so maybe my sons would like to come and camp during the summer. The logs are intact, but everything is down to nothing.

We lived there quite a bit. We didn't have no inside toilets, so we had to go out. We had our house, a garage, and then there was the toilet *(outhouse)* that my dad built. And this [barbed wire fence] used to cross from the top of the hill and it would go all the way, until it crossed the river, and to the next hill.

One time, mother [told my brothers], "You had better go to the bathroom now, before you go to bed." So, they went out and one was standing outside and then the other was inside, one would wait for the other. My brother M____ heard the [fence], you know, "squeak." He turned around and looked up towards where the road is. And that wire, like I told you, that barbed wire goes all the way across, down the ditch, the meadow, and all that. So my brother M____ turned and leaned against the bathroom...that toilet...and told [my other brother] F____, "Hurry! Hurry! There's somebody running down here. Hurry!"

It was a real tall man, but he wouldn't stop to jump over fences. Wherever the fence crossed he would just go *through* it! And my brother M____ stood there looking at him, and he said, "Hurry, there's a man running!"

And then they watched him. My brother F____ had come out and watched him. He went down the little hill we had and there was a wire to cross in the meadow. And he went right through that one too and made noise, like somebody went "ZIP" right through a wire. They heard him until he passed the last [fence] over there and the wires would shake. But he never answered them, and it was a tall man.

The story my grandpa told us was, "When ever you see something like that it's called 'The Wandering Jew.' In Spanish it's called, 'El Judio Errante.' Because that man, they claim, killed his family years and years and years ago. He killed his mother, his dad, his wife and his kids. And the Good Lord told him. ' You will not die until the end of the earth. When the world ends you will die. Your punishment is that you will walk, maybe a hundred, thousand times around the world and in every part of the world. That will be your punishment. You will walk, walk, walk! And when you stop you will hear a voice that says, 'Anda, maldito, anda!' "

And that was the story my grandpa told.

My brother M____ said, "That had to be him! Because he wouldn't stop for wires, he wouldn't jump over a fence, he just went right through it and the wires would make a funny noise!"

My mother said, "We've never heard of anything like that around here."

And my grandpa said, "Well, why not? 'Cause if it was that man walking, and the punishment is to walk until the day the world ends, he has to walk. And a voice will tell him, 'you keep on walking! Walk, walk, walk!' And he would keep on going."

My grandpa came from New Mexico, and he [knew] a lot of things that happened among the Indians, and things that he actually saw himself. "I'm not lying," he would tell me. "I'm not lying."

So, maybe it is true.

H. J. September 1, 2001

First mentioned in a 1602 German pamphlet, the "Wandering Jew" is said to have been a Jerusalem shoemaker named Ahasuerus, cursed by God to perpetually wander the Earth after driving Christ from his door.

39. "DEATH CAME TO SEE HER"

Early 1940's

My mother and I were alone...alone up the canyon. My brother used to take us to get groceries every Saturday. You see, I didn't drive, my mother didn't either. I was with her, the rest [of the family] were gone. *(The storyteller's father and grandparents had passed away when she was young. Her older sister was married, four of her brothers were in the military and a fifth brother lived in Trinidad).*

In the later part of September, I got a real bad pain from the calf to my ankles. One morning I woke up and it looked like I had a ribbon tied [to my ankles]. My feet were not swollen and my legs wasn't, but right there *(the calves)*. I had never complained to my mom, being a young girl I didn't want to say anything. And alone up there, who was gonna take me to the doctor?

One morning I got up and [my legs] were purple. My mom said, "C'mon, get out of bed and help me."

And I told my mom, "I can't!"

She said, "Why?"

And I said, "Well, look at my legs. I can't walk!"

She said, "Oh my God! What am I gonna do? Alone up the canyon, your brother's working at the courthouse *(in Trinidad)* and I don't know how the hell to get word down there!"

Finally, she got me up on a chair. I rested there, lifted my legs up and nothing happened. Then at night I went to bed. Next morning there were about four, like chicken pox, but big ones. Four on one leg and five on the other one, and just from my knees down. My mother said, "I have to walk five miles down the road and call on that phone and tell your brother to come, so he can see you."

And I told my mom, "But I'm gonna be alone here."

She said, "Well, you can't walk."

I don't know if you know North Fork Canyon? You come all the way down to the first filling station, that's how far my mom had to walk. And she walked back up and said, "Your brother's gonna be up here tonight and he's going to take you down."

And I said, "Will you go down with me?"

And she said, "Well, we'll see."

So, I know that he came up, they took me down, but I don't remember what the doctor did or nothing, you know.

Anyway, I was [back home] in bed resting, with my feet elevated. My mom's bed was in a wall.... like that.... and mine was right next to her. We had no screen doors; we slept with the doors open. We could hear all kind of animals out there and my mother was so afraid. And I sure as hell couldn't run!

I was looking out the door, you know. It was about eleven o'clock, and I could hear my mom had prayed and the lights were off. And I could hear that she was kind of snoring.

I was trying to sleep but couldn't sleep at all when I was like that. I looked out the door and I saw a shadow. It walked up the stairs and came in. And this lady...to me it was a lady...she had her arms like this (crossed). She had a hood, but no face. She looked this way, and that way, and then looked at me. I never saw a face. It was just the motion, you know. She was dressed in black and tall...real skinny and tall.

She came and knelt by my bed, I still never saw a face. And with her arms [crossed] she bent down and kissed me right here (on the forehead). And it was cold! Cold! That I remember. It was cold. And she got up, looked around and walked out. When she was walking out, I laughed, you know.

"Ma! Maaa!"

"What?"

"Who was that lady? Who was that lady that came?

And my mom got scared and she said, "What lady?"

And I said, "She's going down the stairs!"

My mom got up, went out there...went around the house...came back, and she said, "Are you hallucinating, or what's wrong with you? There was no lady!"

"Yes there was ma!" And I laughed. She thought I was making a joke. To me it was funny that she didn't see nobody, so I laughed.

Next day, when my brother came, she was nervous.... she was crying. And [my brother] said, "Well maybe, mamma, she was just dreaming. Maybe nothing like that happened."

I said, "But I was awake! I could hear you snoring ma. And you had finished praying. But she did come!"

"Well, what did she look like?"

I had a godmother that baptized me, that was real tall and lanky. She must have been six feet tall...maybe more. And

I said, "She was built like my godmother."

And my mother said, "For God's sake, your godmother's been dead for a long time!"

I said, "Okay. But that's what she looked like. "

[My mother] got scared, she'd watch me day and night. Pretty soon we had Mass up in Vigil. By that time I was ready to walk a little bit, so we walked to church. And my mom said, "I have to talk to the priest." It didn't dawn on me or anything at the time. That was her business. She didn't tell me anything until we got home. And I said, "How come you talked to the priest, ma?"

She said, "What do you mean?"

I said, "Well, you talked to him. You said you were going to talk to him."

"Oh, do you really want to know?"

And I said, "Yes. You talked to him about me, didn't you?

And she said, "Yes I did."

I said, "But why ma?"

"Because I want to know the truth!"

I said, "Okay. What did he tell you?"

[The priest] told her, "Death came to see her that night, but didn't want to take her. That's what it is and that is what you should believe."

I never got scared, my mother cried and everything. And I said, "Well, I didn't die!"

I was not hallucinating, you know, I was just lying there with my feet propped up. I didn't have a fever, but I did see that. God only knows what it was.

H. J. September 1, 2001

40. "THE DEVIL IS LOOSE AT MIDNIGHT"

You know, my sister-in-law used to go at nine o'clock at night and open the church, that little Vigil Church. They had an organ and she'd go and practice and sing.

One time she said, "I didn't realize it was twelve o'clock at night. [A] horrible thing happened to me. I don't know if it was horrible, or saints, or what!"

She used to leave the doors partly open, so she wouldn't get locked out. And that night she was playing, never realizing that it was twelve o'clock at night. Her dad used to tell her, "If you don't get out of there by midnight, you're gonna have an experience you're not gonna believe!"

And she said, "I laughed at him, 'cause what does my daddy know?"

She was playing when all of a sudden, the two doors opened. A wind...so strong...came in and went around twice and knocked her books from the organ. She took off and closed the door. She said, "Whatever came in stayed in there, 'cause I locked the door and I went home!"

She told her daddy and he said, "I told you that the devil is loose at midnight, and that's where he went!"

She said it was the most horrible wind, that the doors just opened and the wind came in.

H. J. September 1, 2001

Vigil is a small Spanish settlement located along Highway 12, about 30 miles west of Trinidad.

41. FOG

1957

I was married at the time and living in Weston. I was visiting this lady and I stayed kind of late. She lived right in front of the [train] tracks...you had to come down the road and come to a little alley there. Anyway, it got late and one of her boys was drunker than hell.

I said, "Well, I'm gonna go home."

And she said, "Aren't you afraid?"

And I said, "Well, I am a little afraid of the dogs, but I'll make it okay. I'll call you when I get home to the end of Weston.

When we went out, she walked out with me... and her son [was] standing with us, drunker than hell... and I said, "What is that thing coming down the tracks?" It was like a ball of transparent foam, like, like,...fog. And it was coming down the tracks, down towards Weston.

We both stood there and when it got close...like from here to there...you could see through [it]. But it was a lady just waving her arms and wearing like a veil, you know, and just floating...floating down the tracks.

And I told her *(the friend)*, "What in the world was that?" She said,...she said some kind of name, you know.

And I said, "Well, I never heard of that before. But look at her, she's not touching the ground!" And then like a mist, she disappeared down below Weston.

And then another time I saw the same thing, as I was crossing the tracks with one of my brothers. I looked and I thought. "Oh no, not again!"

And here comes that lady, right by me, you know, in

front of me like that, just floating. Then she went, into thin air.

And now I'm not the only one who saw this, there were three or four people. One man got sober and he quit drinking!

Oh God, it was scary!

H. J. March 28, 2001

Once the "center of a great timber region," Weston, located along the famed "Highway of Legends" (Highway 12), is today a quiet village about 22 miles west of Trinidad.

42. BLACK, LIKE A CLOUD

And then they talk about the *Llorona*. And that one, I don't know if it was a fox or if it was the *Llorona* or what.

I lived right here by the river (the Purgatoire) in Weston, before you cross the bridge coming down. My kids and I had been standing there a long time and I told them, "It's getting late, you guys had better go in."

And they said, "No mamma, we're gonna play a little while."

And I said, "The *Llorona's* gonna get you!" You know, just playing. When all of a sudden we heard this cry. My grandpa used to say that a fox would cry like that, they would put their nose down and cry. But this wasn't the cry of a fox; it was the cry of a lady. Like if you could close your eyes and follow, you know, down the river and under the bridge and all the way down. And then she stopped.

The next day I went to visit one of the ladies and I told her, "Did you hear that coyote last night?"

And she said, "That was no coyote."

And I said, "Well, it had to be a fox."

And she said, "That was no fox."

I said, "Well, what in the hell was it?"

She said, "We've heard that cry before, many years ago."

And I said, "It's like *Llorona*? That happened in Mexico, not here."

She said, "I don't know. But you haven't seen her float, black, like a cloud, down the river."

And it was a wail, just like if a lady cry "EEEEEEE," and then *(sobbing noises)* and then it stopped.

And you shivered, because you know it was a lady crying for something. It was weird.

H. J. March 28, 2001

43. "THEY FORGOT TO TURN THE CANDLES OFF"

I don't know if the ladies...the women of Weston...saw it, but this man reported that at a certain time of the week at a certain hour, the church in Weston would light up, you know, and there was no mass or nothing in there.

So one time my son and I were coming [home] and we could see a candle on in the church. And I told him, "I wonder who's in there? They forgot to turn the candles off."

He says, "I dunno mamma, but let me park here."

I was right next to the church in Weston, that's where I lived. And I went over [to the church] and everything went pitch black.

But coming up the road you could see a light in the window. There was a candle! They say no, nobody was there. But I did go and see, and I didn't get scared. The minute I didn't find no candle, I went home!

They say that a lot of times they would see a light. Older people...way older than I...that lived in Weston a long time, they have seen that. But, I dunno, that's the only thing I saw. It was about eleven o'clock at night... and who could've been lighting that candle? I even tried the door, it was locked.

But, there's a lot of things, you know. Maybe somebody wants some forgiveness for something. I believe in that.

H. J. March 28, 2001

44. PEOPLE COMING DOWN THE STAIRS

That house I lived in, they said there were a lot of bad memories in that house. And it wouldn't happen when my kids were around, only one of my boys.

We went to bed, and I laid down [in the other room], and my son said, "Mamma, there goes that noise again!"

See, it had an upstairs and they claimed someone was killed in that house. You could hear steps going all the way down. But when it got to the bottom step, you open the door to see what was there and there wasn't nothing there! That happened about four or five times.

I told my boy, "Well, get up and see."

He said, "Hell no mamma, I ain't gonna get up!"

And I said, "Well, why?"

And I got up and looked around and the noise would stop. Then the moment I went [across the room], it started again! People coming down the stairs. But it was real. It couldn't have been a mouse or a bat. It wasn't. It had a heavy step.

That was right here in Weston. You know where that big garage is right across [from] the store? There was a two-story house there that I lived [in]. That's when I divorced and had to take my family there.

Oh, and they'd whistle! You'd be in bed and they'd whistle. You would swear somebody was standing by the stove. I'd get up and the doors were locked, but you would lay down and they'd go *"FFT, FFT,"* you know, loud!

I said, "It's outside."

And [my son] said, "Mamma it's not outside, it's in the house."

And I said, "Let it go, I'm tired!"

H. J. March 28, 2001

45. "IT'S MY EYES"

Just the other day, right they're in my house...this house, we just bought it, oh, I'd say about twenty years I've lived here (*Segundo*), I've raised my family here.

Twice I've been sitting down crocheting and I...I tell my son..."It's my eyes."

He says, "Mamma, how can it be your eyes all the time?"

I see something out of the corner of my eye, like floating from the kitchen into the bedroom. And [I] try sometime to get up and follow it, but when I get there there's nothing there.

And the people who lived there before...this lady told me this...she would see somebody, like somebody go really fast into the kitchen, then into the bathroom and turn real fast. But there was nobody there. And I told her I get the feeling when I go to bed that I'm not alone.

She said, "Well, my mom did too! I told her, it's not scary."

And I said, "But I have a feeling that there's somebody there. Either by my side, or like going in from one room to another, you know."

There are times it will give me a little chill, but I would say, "Oh God, there's nothing in here, I know there isn't." But, I don't know what it is. That's something I guess we'll never know.

And this lady lived there and she said they never had any problems. But her mother was always saying, "You know, I have a feeling that there's somebody else in this house with me."

And my grandpa used to believe in [these] things. He [said], "Pray for whatever souls you think, because they may be wandering and want your forgiveness." So that's what I think.

H. J. March 28, 2001